LIONS

Lions
in the
Animal World

The adult male lion is easily recognizable by his thick mane; but his most fascinating characteristic is perhaps the extraordinary colour of his large, amber eyes.

The most handsome cat

With his splendid mane and lofty bearing, his supple, muscular body and terrifying roar, the lion has always been known as 'king of the beasts' and 'lord of the steppes'. Feared and fearsome, he is among the largest predators on the planet.

Solitary lions are few on the savannah; lions are the only felines to live in social groups. Even single young males band together.

W ith his green-gold eyes and royal mane, the supple movements of his powerful body, his fine tawny coat and a roar that shakes the earth itself, the lion is a magnificent and awesome feline. His roar and thick mane distinguish the adult male lion from other big cats, such as tigers or leopards. After the tiger, the lion is the largest feline on earth. The male 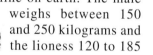 weighs between 150 and 250 kilograms and the lioness 120 to 185

The lion uses his roar to assert his dominance.

From the age of 14 weeks, young lion cubs start to learn hunting skills by watching the techniques the lionesses use in their search for food.

A glance at the lion's majestic face makes it possible to tell individuals apart by the position of the markings on each animal's muzzle.

The male lion prowls the African savannah.

kilograms. The adult male is large, measuring 2.6 to 3.3 metres including his tail; the female is smaller, between 2.4 and 2.7 metres. Of all species of cat, the lion is the one with the greatest size and weight differentials (20 to 50 percent) between males and females.

A savannah-coloured coat

Lions also differ from their cousins the tigers, leopards, jaguars and other big cats because of their coat, which may vary in colour from silvery yellow to dark brown. Lion cubs usually have short, pale-coloured fur, dappled with dark brown. As the cub grows older the colours merge into a beautiful golden tawny, a colour described as 'mimetic', since it imitates the colour of the long grasses of the African savannah to camouflage the lions. Sometimes the darker 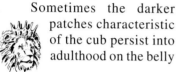 patches characteristic of the cub persist into adulthood on the belly

Lion cubs start to walk 10 to 15 days after birth.

The male lion can be up to twice as heavy as the female. He is stronger, but less active than his mate.

Exhausted, but satisfied, the lioness rests after her long night's hunting. In the golden light of dawn, her large, honey-coloured eyes seem filled with a fiery light.

Although its early years are spent in the harsh struggle for survival, the lion cub is a very playful and lively young animal.

After feeding, lions abandon their kill and go off to drink.

and inner thigh, particularly on the coats of lionesses.

Manes: an effective deterrent

The mane starts to grow when the young male is about two years old and starts off pale in colour. On lions of five or six years old, it may reach a length of more than 20 centimetres and tends to darken, from back to front, varying from pale tawny to red, brown or black. Not all male lions have this virile

The supple, slender lioness is both an attentive mother and a highly skilled hunter, who maintains the whole family by providing their daily food ration.

attribute, whose colour and thickness differ from individual to individual: some manes are long, covering the top of the head, the cheeks, neck, shoulders, chest and belly; some are short, simply surrounding the face and neck. The mane acts as a very effective deterrent and the greater its volume, the more it impresses an enemy. During fights between rival males it also softens any blows to the head and neck.

The young lion still has a thin mane, which grows thicker with age.

Lionesses, lions and cubs regularly sharpen their long retractable claws, which can cut like a razor.

Like all felines, from the wildest to the most domesticated, lions carefully wash themselves every day, sometimes as a group.

The Atlas lions and those of Cape Province, which are now extinct, had an extraordinarily full, dark mane. The last remaining Indian lions also have dark manes, but these are less developed than those of their African cousins.

Terrible claws

Lions, like most cats, have fearsome weapons on their paws: curved, pointed claws which may grow to a length

The lion's powerful jaws enable it to tear its victims to pieces.

of 10 centimetres. These terrible daggers enable them to hold their prey down while they administer the death blow with their teeth. Lions retract their claws for walking and extend them to attack. When the lion is resting, its claws are hidden in a skin sheath, giving the animal 'velvet paws'.

Well-adapted teeth

The lion feeds lying down. It grasps strips of its prey's flesh in its short jaws and tears them off with a quick movement of its head. The lion's mouth is better adapted for tearing its victims to pieces than for chewing and contains extremely impressive teeth: canines about 6 centimetres long, short, sharp incisors and what are called 'carnassial' teeth, which enable the animal to mince up meat. This particularly well designed dentition corresponds to the lion's purely carnivorous diet.

A fly-swatter for a tail

The lion's tail, between 60 centimetres and a metre long, ends in a very thick tuft of

A very full mane is a sure sign of a lion's virility.

To give its prodigious roar, the lion bares its jaws with their imposing canines: this 'big mouth' has some pretty persuasive arguments!

▼ We still do not know why the mane varies so much in volume and thickness from individual to individual and from species to species. It could be a matter of heredity, like the differences in hair quantity among human beings. It has also been suggested that lions living in denser brush lose their longer hairs by constantly pushing through thorny bushes. The fact that lions in captivity generally develop thicker, more complete manes supports this hypothesis.

Lazy and indolent by day, at night the lion is transformed into a ruthless hunter. Dusk is greeted by deep roars and heralds the long night's chase.

It is at sunset that lions roar the most. The animal stands with its head bowed, pulls in its sides and swells its chest. Its powerful exhalation sometimes makes the dust swirl. This roaring is not intended to frighten prey, as has often been claimed; zebras and gazelles never take flight on hearing it. It is to tell any intruders that the territory is occupied.

The colour of the lion's iris varies with individuals from gold to brown.

hair, which hides a horny excrescence up to 10 millimetres long and shaped like a dog's dewclaw. In an attempt to drive away the flies whose constant incursions undermine its royal image, the lion whips this tail from side to side. Tail movements may also express anger and bad temper. The idea that an angry lion beats itself with the 'claw' at the end of its tail before moving to attack is unfounded. This claw is simply a small piece of horn attached to the skin at the end of the last vertebra.

The lion's evening roar deep in the savannah

The lion is the only feline to roar, by vibrating an elastic ligament in its jaw as it breathes out. Its roar is said to be the most terrifying and imposing of all wild animal calls. In the right conditions it can be heard for 10 kilometres all around. Lions roar in the evening, when they are getting ready to hunt, and at dawn, before they go to rest.

The lion is at the top of the food chain and may devour up to 20 kilograms of meat a day in preparation for times of scarcity.

A fearsome predator

With its carnivorous diet and, huge appetite, the lion is a powerful killer roaming the savannah, a hunter that most animals fear. However it kills only for food and in so doing helps maintain the balance of nature.

At the point of leaping on her prey, a lioness may be moving at 40 to 60 kph. Though this is a good speed, it gives her no margin for error.

The male lion, king of the beasts, dominates the savannah, regarding the species that surround him with a certain indifference. When his majesty is hungry, any subject in his path becomes a potential kill. Like all big cats, lions are predators at the top of the food chain, although they will also stoop to eat carrion. Lions become active at dusk, and hunt on their own territory all through the night, until dusk.

Sudden acts of ferocity reveal the fierce nature of the lioness.

Lionesses in the same group spend their periods of rest and recreation together, just as they share out the tasks at hunting time.

A buffalo makes a tough opponent for a lion, which generally avoids attacking one on its own. However the presence of buffalo does not bother the king of the beasts.

Strength through unity

On the great African savannah, lions can easily be spotted by their future victims. A vigorous animal such as a buffalo can easily deal with a single lion which will never risk being caught on its horns. For this reason lions, being brave but not foolhardy, hunt in pairs or groups, which gives them a better chance of success and enables them to try for a larger kill. Lions belonging

The lion is a super-predator, fearing no animal on the savannah.

to the same clan will also get together to sortie into the savannah at night. At least one female stays at base camp with the cubs and a few males stand guard, ready to drive away any intruders.

The lazy king puts his lionesses to work

Lions hunt primarily by lying in wait for their prey and surrounding it. Most hunting is done by females, who are faster, more agile and better at staying hidden than their regal husbands. Their favourite prey is the gnu, which takes first place on the menu, followed by the zebra. These powerful cats also attack smaller prey, such as antelopes and baboons; but when a lion is hungry it will try its luck with an animal much larger than itself, such as a buffalo or a giraffe, usually without much success. The only animals a lion will not attempt to kill are adult elephants and rhinoceroses; these giants from another time are so much bigger that the cat would be bound to fail.

Lions do not like effort, preferring to sprawl in the shade.

The lion's hunting instinct never sleeps, even during the animal's long rest periods. Its highly sensitive senses of hearing and smell are always on the alert.

▼ In the savannah, the activities of lions and other predators help to keep down the numbers of herbivores such as gnus and zebras. In this way they prevent overpopulation, which could lead to the rapid destruction of vegetation and a serious risk of desertification. In addition, this natural regulation culls the slowest, least agile and least attentive animals, in other words those least well-equipped for survival. Lions thus contribute to natural selection, which maintains the health and strength of herds.

A young elephant calf is defenceless against determined lions, who seize any opportunity for feeding.

Radical technique

Lions like to hunt at dawn or at dusk, when they are perfectly camouflaged by their tawny coats. At night they are still fearsome hunters, as their eyes adapt to the darkness. Lurking in the long grass, they wait until their prey gives signs of inattention, is too busy grazing or becomes isolated. Once the victim has been chosen, the lion leaps forward with great

The power of the lion's charge is the key element in successful hunting.

Although the lionesses do his hunting for him, the male lion is just as ruthless a killer when the need arises.

After stunning his prey with a blow from his paw, then killing it by a bite to the throat, the lion quickly devours his victim's warm flesh.

power and speed. The unlucky prey has very little chance of escape if the lion reaches it. After pulling it violently to the ground, the lion lies on it with its full weight and seizes it by the throat. Once its trachea and oesophagus are cut, the animal will die within a few minutes. If, on the other hand, it evades the lion's first attack, it has a good chance of survival, depending on how fast it can run. Lions do not have a great deal of stamina

The lion's savage nature is revealed when it gorges on its victim's flesh.

One of the lion's favourite victims is the gnu, a peaceable, good-natured herbivore. Lions often use the cover of darkness to surprise a gnu while it is drinking at a waterhole.

When the lion has finished with a carcass, it leaves the remains of its meal to the vultures and hyenas, who pick the skeleton completely clean.

▼ Sharing out the kill may give rise to spectacular quarrels, depending on the size of the carcass and the lions' hunger. In times of abundance on the African savannah, the struggle for food is less intense and even the lion cubs eat their fill. The dry season is often a time of scarcity when lions fight bitterly over the smallest scrap of meat, with no concern for family ties. At such times mothers will knock their hungry cubs aside.

The claws of the attacking lioness do serious damage.

and almost always abandon the chase. When hunting in groups of more than three, lions often encircle their prey. They move together towards a group of potential victims, then discreetly split up. Some crouch down to lie in wait in the long grass, downwind of the game. The others approach the prey openly, frightening them into thoughtless flight towards the killers, who simply have to intercept them in order to make the kill.

Eating carrion when necessary

Since only a quarter of their attempts to kill succeed, lions, being entirely carnivorous, do not feast every day. However they have a ferocious appetite, needing 7 kilograms of meat daily to stave off their hunger. This means they cannot afford to be fussy eaters. In times of scarcity they eat animals that have died of sickness, or else the remains left behind by other, luckier predators. It is thus not uncommon to see lions turn to eating carrion and fighting over a carcass with hyenas. For want of

Lion cubs practise the art of hunting from a very young age. Simulated chases develop their agility, speed and aggression.

The lion's greed is increased by the frequent failure of its attacks.

better prey, when the herbivores have mostly migrated in search of water, lions will attack small mammals, birds, snakes and even crocodiles.

The lion's share

In normal circumstances the prey caught by the lionesses is shared out among all the members of their pride. As often happens in nature, the largest shares go to the strongest animals, so that big males who have not participated in the hunt are often the first to gorge themselves. These profiteers, confident of their strength, seize the fresh kill – hence the common phrase 'the lion's share'. When there is not enough room for the whole pride to eat together side by side, the males eat first. Once they have finished, the adult lionesses have their turn at the carcass. The young males and the cubs have to wait until last.

When a lion cub gets its share of a meal, it savours even the tiniest morsel.

A floating hippopotamus carcass makes a highly acceptable meal for lions, who happily eat carrion when game is scarce.

The male lion's reputation for laziness is only partly deserved. Although males spend a lot of time resting, they have to work hard to defend their territory.

A lazy king on a vulnerable throne

Lions differ from other cats in that they live in groups or prides. This guarantees the safety of all group members in a fiercely defended territory. The sharing of kills also ensures that all can survive. However, the battles fought between males for control of the clan are merciless.

A group of lionnesses, consisting of mothers, daughters, sisters and cousins, forms a large, close-knit family who educate their little cubs together.

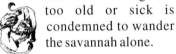

Lions live in large social groups in which the females and their cubs maintain a coherent family structure. The dominant males, lazy kings whose power is fragile, divide their time between patrolling their territory and taking long rests. Their lionesses are responsible for most of the hunting and keep the whole family provided with fresh meat. A male that grows too old or sick is condemned to wander the savannah alone.

An old male faces a future of solitary wandering.

Like all big cats, lions enjoy long periods of leisure lasting between 20 and 21 hours a day, of which 10 to 15 hours are spent sleeping.

Lionnesses live collectively, supporting each other in their social life and cooperating in the hunt, when their combined strength makes them more effective.

Close-knit families

In each pride related lionesses form a highly stable family core: mothers and daughters stay in the same group all their lives, hunting and bringing up their young together. Thus an average pride contains about 15 animals, including males and cubs. This number may vary with time however, depending on the availability of game in the territory. Moreover, the male lions are

The cubs are still weak and are only really safe within the group.

Young male lions seeking power form alliances with others of their own age to try and take over a pride controlled by one dominant male.

never seen as permanent in the pride – lionesses agree to receive and feed only the strongest males.

Nomadic lions

If young males have not spontaneously left their family group by the age of three-and-a-half, they are driven away by their mother and her fellow lionesses. They generally leave in groups in two or three of the same age, and

The cruelty of the wild does not rule out moments of peaceful family life.

Mistress of all she surveys, the lioness bows to no other animal on the savannah, not even her mate, whom she delegates to defend their territory.

The male lion dominates his territory less by direct confrontation with his rivals than by his roar, which gives a sonorous warning to all.

become nomads until they are strong enough to fight for position with other males.

A ruthless power struggle

Despite their image as lazy animals leaving all the work to their females, large adult male lions actively guard their territory. They mark their dominance with terrible roars and judiciously aimed jets of urine, while wherever possible repelling any intruder who wants to

The male and female lions may have a harmonious, if temporary, relationship.

The dominant male in a pride reigns over a harem of lionesses. In return he protects both them and himself from ill-intentioned rivals.

challenge their ephemeral glory. However, this behaviour has its dangers, since all around the pride young lions are wandering in search of power and constantly watching for any sign of weakness or old age in the dominant males in order to usurp their coveted role. In the face of such competition, dominant males keep their position of control in a pride for only two to four years, after which they are driven away,

The lion's haughty bearing asserts his dominance over the territory.

When a fight for power becomes inevitable, males may give each other dangerous and sometimes fatal injuries with their paws and teeth.

Like many other cats, large and small, lions mark out their territory by urinating on stones and tree-stumps, leaving distinctive signs.

The violence of the struggle for power can leave painful scars.

injured or even killed by a new alliance of males asserting their power.

Masculine rivalry

On the arrival of an unknown male, the pride's males try to avoid a fight. By means of intimidatory displays, they quickly gauge the strength of their opponent, who beats a hasty retreat if he feels at too much of a disadvantage. When it comes to a fight, however, manes come into

The lioness in heat parades before the male, rolling on the ground to make it obvious to her future partner that she is ready to accept his advances.

The male carefully sniffs his partner to check that she is on heat.

their own: apart from the effect of their volume, which makes the lions look bigger than they really are, they successfully deaden blows. Nevertheless, in a violent struggle between two opponents of similar strength, there is a genuine risk of serious injury and even death.

A lion and a lioness

Love among the lions lasts all year round: mating is not restricted to a particular

The male lion gently holds the female's neck in his mouth, just as the mother lioness holds her cub by the skin on its neck when moving it from place to place.

The parade which precedes mating is a kind of sophisticated dance, during which the female offers herself to, then rejects, the male, stirring up his lust.

season and outside gestation and nursing periods, lionesses regularly come on heat for a period of between four and eight days. At this time couples form and go a little way from the group to mate. The whole day is spent in preparatory caresses and initial attempts at coupling, which are usually unsuccessful. The obstinate male stays with his lioness and his presence keeps all the other males at a respectable distance.

For lions the fiercely impressive act of mating is very intense.

Lions mate up to 50 times a day. If the lioness does not become pregnant she comes on heat again one to three months later.

It takes a small miracle for a lioness to become pregnant. Lions have a very low rate of reproduction, obliging them to mate a great many times.

▼ A lioness often nurses other cubs beside her own; it is common for cubs with different mothers to feed together from the same lioness. This sharing of maternal tasks is typical of the species, unlike other mammals, whose females look after only their own young. Female lions may even adopt orphaned young cubs into their pride. To ensure fairness, a lioness will feed the smallest cubs first, even when they do not belong to her. The larger ones have to wait.

Love games

As a prelude to mating, the male and female lion rub their heads together and take great pleasure in sniffing each other's genitals. The lioness presents her hindquarters, then moves away. She rolls on to her back, gets up again and trots away for about 50 metres, before lying down again in an elaborate game of seduction. This dance may continue for over half an hour, during which the male assiduously courts his partner, unconcerned when she cuffs him with her claws drawn in.

Lions may mate up to 50 times in one day.

The queen always gives herself in pain

When the lioness is at last ready to give herself to her partner, she approaches him with a low growl. Mating itself lasts barely ten seconds, during which the male grips the female's neck firmly between his teeth, but without biting her. He quickly withdraws when the female groans, threatening to strike him with her paw or bite him. There is no violence in the act of mating; however

some zoologists believe that the lioness may at one point feel a sharp pain, which they think sets off the ovulation process which must occur if she is to become pregnant.

A royal temperament

Lions may mate up to 50 times in 24 hours: for a single female in heat this may mean every 15 minutes. If a female is not impregnated, she will come on heat again one to three months later. Despite the great frequency of reproductive activity, the lion's chances of procreation remain poor: there is only one birth for every five periods on heat, or for every 1000 couplings.

The lioness is an attentive mother whose cubs are vulnerable to predators.

The lioness is a real 'mother hen'

After a gestation period of 110 days, the lioness gives birth to a litter of between two and four cubs weighing less than 2 kilograms at birth. Their eyes do not open for 10 to 15 days and they are not really able to move around before they are three weeks old. At first the female keeps her young away from the rest of

The lioness nurses her cubs for about six months, unless they are brutally killed, as often happens when a young male seizes control of the pride.

▼ Despite the lionesses' care, barely 20 percent of a pride's lion cubs make it to adulthood. A quarter of the deaths are due to undernourishment: the cubs have to use all kinds of cunning tricks to obtain a few scraps of meat, particularly in times of scarcity. The other factor explaining this high infant mortality rate is the behaviour of adult males, who readily kill cubs they did not father, particularly when they first take over control of a pride.

the pride, in a rocky shelter, a thicket or among the long grasses. She is highly protective of her litter and keeps constant watch. Always fearing the arrival of predators such as hyenas or vultures, she moves her cubs one by one, carrying them in her mouth. When the cubs grow bigger, the lionesses share the care of the cubs and take turns in playing with them. Almost all the young in a pride grow up together.

The cub learns the art of hunting while out with its mother.

The lioness moves her cubs one by one, gently grasping their shoulders in her mouth. She changes their hiding place about every three days during their first weeks.

Male lions are very tolerant fathers. Their cubs give them lots of caresses, which seems to disarm their aggression.

So young and already a hunter

Ten weeks after they are born, the cubs join the rest of the pride with their mother and share the life of the adult females and other cubs. From the age of 14 weeks, they start learning how to hunt by following the females. At a year old they can herd prey, and at two years they are confident enough to embark on hunting alone.

Lion cubs climb trees, learning how to lie in wait before attacking.

The coveted title of largest living cat belongs to the tigers of Asia such as this Siberian tiger, which have withstood the changes to their natural habitat better than the lion.

Fierce ancestors
and extinct cousins

Lions used to be one of the most widely
distributed wild beasts on earth, but their
numbers have dwindled as human civilization has
spread. The Cape lion, the Iranian lion and the Atlas
lion have completely disappeared, while the last lions
in Asia survive in the Gir nature reserve in India.

The last of the Asiatic lions, magnificent animals which were once worshipped, are now
reduced to precarious survival in the protected Gir national park in India.

Today the most widespread population of tigers is that of the Bengal tiger: an estimated 4000 still roam the rainforests of India.

The cosmopolitan leopard can be found in both Africa and Asia.

The king of the beasts has been unrelentingly hunted and numbers have dwindled as new weapons have been developed. Lion populations were decimated in the 19th century with the appearance of modern guns, and lions have gradually disappeared from places where they had been feared for thousands of years.

Lost lions

The Balkan lion, last descendant of the cave

lion that thrived in Europe during the last Ice Age, can be traced in the works of the Ancients. More recently, the Persian lion definitively disappeared around 1830. The last of the Atlas lions was killed in Morocco in 1920. The Cape lion, with its fine black mane, was exterminated in the 1870s. The Transvaal lion also succumbed to hunters. In the Sahara the lion is now only a distant memory and the species is currently vanishing from the countries of the Sahel.

The puma, the lion's distant cousin, is found throughout the Americas.

The territory of the jaguar, American equivalent of the leopard, extends from the southern United States to Argentina, but has been considerably diminished.

The cave lion, prehistoric ancestor of today's lions, fascinated the first human beings, who often depicted it in their cave paintings.

The sabre-toothed tiger existed from the Oligocene era to the Pleistocene. They were named after their long, sharp upper canines. These carnivores inhabited a wide area: specimens have been found in Eurasia and Africa. A giant form, the Smilodon, was found in America and was considerably larger than the lions of today. It disappeared around 10,000 years ago.

Prehistoric lions

Miacis, the most distant ancestor of not only lions but also dogs, is the earliest known carnivore. It populated Earth 40 million years ago. This primitive little animal, with short legs and a long tail, probably lived in the trees. Ten million years later, Nimravinae, another venerable ancestor of the lion, was already the proud owner of proper feline dentition, with long, sharp canines. Many times in the history of this fearsome family, the canines have grown longer and thinner, to the point where they overhang the lower jaw. The terrible Smilodon, better-known as the giant sabre-toothed tiger, was the last representative of these cats with long canines and died out 10,000 years ago.

The legendary sabre-toothed tiger remains an enigma.

Cave lions

Since then, many fossil populations of the direct ancestors of today's lion, *panthera leo*, have been found: *Panthera atrox* in America and *Panthera spelaea* in Europe. *Panthera spelaea*, also known as the cave lion, is depicted in rock paintings in the Combarelles caves in the Dordogne region of southern France. These paintings date from the Upper Palaeolithic (13,000–8000 years BC).

When the predator becomes the prey

In Antiquity, lions still inhabited a very wide area, including all of Africa, south-eastern Europe, the Middle East, Asia Minor and eastwards into India; but they were excessively

When attacking, the smilodon used its enormous canines like daggers.

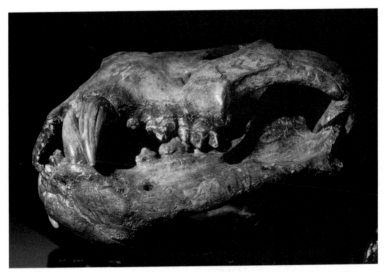

The cave lion, closely related to modern lions, lived in Europe more than 100 000 years ago. A cousin of similar size was to be found in North America.

A family photo of the cats alive today, from the lion to the domestic tabby, including the wild cat, lynx, leopard, jaguar and tiger.

No big pussycat, the lion is the proud representative of the larger felines.

hunted and today the last surviving specimens are found only in the African national parks and one Indian nature reserve.

The last lions of Asia

The hundred or so lions confined to the Gir forest in Gujarat in India are all that remain of an immense population that once thrived as far east as Bengal. Deforestation and the cultivation of vast tracts of virgin land have considerably reduced the natural territory of the Asian lion. As game became more scarce, lions died of starvation. Their only alternative was to feed on the animals kept by humans, who then saw them only as a problem to be eliminated. The sociable, lazy and incautious lions suffered more than their prestigious cousin the tiger. Today the Asian lion has lost much of its glory, being confined to one small forest, where it is protected.

An uncertain future

Many studies carried out by the Indian authorities in collaboration with the World Wildlife Fund have identified the fundamental game requirements of the Gir lions. Following action to deal with the threat of desertification in the zone due to the overconsumption of forest resources by her- bivores, the vegetation and wild animal populations have returned to normal. The last Indian lions were thus assured the minimum necessary for their survival. Unfortunately their isolation makes them vulnerable to the slightest epidemic and, in the longer

Last survivor of a dwindling dynasty, the Asiatic lion survives as best it can.

The hungry tiger is a ruthless carnivore, whose ferocity, appetite and infallible predatory instincts equal those of the lion.

In 1947 there were about 200 Asiatic lions in Gir, in the Indian state of Gujarat. At this time the Indian authorities designated the Gir National Park as a nature reserve where the last living specimens would be protected. Today the Gir National Park is the only place in the world where Asiatic lions can still be seen in the wild. The reserve, covering 1000 square kilometres, also gives protection to leopards, antelopes, deer, jackals, hyenas and crocodiles.

term, the deleterious effects of inbreeding.

The lion's cousins

The lion (*Panthera leo*) is one of four species in the Panthera genus, which represents the largest of the cats. The three other club members are the leopard, or panther (*Panthera pardus*), the jaguar (*Panthera onca*) and the tiger (*Panthera tigris*). The discreet leopard inhabits Africa and Asia; the jaguar is found only in the equatorial forests of the Americas, from Mexico

The jaguar is the only representative of the panthera genus in the New World.

The Siberian tiger is the largest living cat and a giant among tigers. Its thick fur enables it to survive in very low winter temperatures.

Puma is the Peruvian name for the American big cat felis concolor. In South America this animal is known as the 'cougar', 'red tiger' or 'leon' (lion).

to northern Argentina; the tiger, considered the largest cat, is a close cousin to the lion: cubs have already been cross-bred in captivity from a tiger and a lioness. Present in all thickly vegetated areas of continental Asia (India, south-east Asia, China, Siberia, Sumatra), the tiger is a discreet animal that can live anywhere where game is plentiful and cover is thick enough for it to hide in. Its striped coat providesd perfect camouflage as it crouches in the shadows ready to pounce on its prey.

The leopard has suffered cruelly as a result of its beautiful coat.

Lions in Our World

The nomadic Masai people of Africa are herdsmen who used to fight lions in single combat. They have given the king of beasts the central place in their ancestral culture.

Lord of his lands in Africa

On the African continent the lion's status is not only mythical; lions are and always have been part of people's everyday lives. The king of the beasts is a major figure in Masai culture and was also a central element in the civilization of Ancient Egypt.

Lions are protected today, but they used to be hunted by herdsmen, whose stock they decimated, and by hunters who would take their skins as trophies.

In Africa the lion embodies royal authority. Yet this king of the beasts is often beaten by smaller, cleverer creatures such as hares and spiders, two animals that are very popular in African myth. In the lands of the eastern and southern savannah, the hare is seen as a sly and cunning character who easily fools the lion, hyena, hippopotamus and elephant. In western and central Africa this role is given to the spider.

The lion is king among both animals and human beings.

Fearsome enemy of both livestock and people and symbol of blind, unthinking force, the lion is ridiculed in traditional African tales.

The fantasy of taming the lion is common among travellers, who are fascinated by the big cat; however in African culture the lion is the enemy of human beings.

The Masai and the lion

The Masai are a fierce people who graze their herds on the savannah of southern Kenya and northern Tanzania. They are nomads in an untamed environment. Since they are entirely dependent on the animals they keep, the Masai learn at an early age to stay on the alert in order not to lose too many of them. Older people teach the younger ones the arts of protecting their own beasts and recognizing most predators (lions,

The Masai warrior is never without his weapon of choice, a lance.

Masai men and women wear traditional headdresses and jewellery. In days gone by young men would wear a lion's mane on completing their initiation rite.

leopards or hyenas) from their tracks and cries. For thousands of years the lions and Masai of Kenya were caught up in a ruthless struggle. The lions were awkward neighbours, taking a cow from time to time from the Masai herds. Sometimes they would even approach a camp and kill a human being. Yet far from giving in to the lions, the Masai herdsmen decided to confront the great beast, armed only with lances and leather shields. Over time this fight became an initiatory

Lions' ferocious appetite is not to the herdsmen's taste.

The traditional culture of the Samburu people of Kenya is very similar to that of the Masai. The Samburu also raise cattle, but have adapted more successfully to modern life.

ordeal, taking on a ritual and truly sacred dimension. In order to attain adulthood a Masai youth had to prove his courage and worth by killing a lion. This was a highly dangerous undertaking, particularly since the Masai had invested the lion with supernatural powers. To eat lion or to wear lion claws, teeth or mane as an ornament was supposed to give the wearer healing powers and even immortality.

During the eunoto celebrations the young Masai warriors become 'elders'.

Joseph Kessel's famous novel The Lion describes the ancestral combat between the Masai warrior and the lion, a contest banned by the white colonisers.

Lance in hand, young Masai take their livestock to graze. The Masai are known for their size - many are two metres tall - and for their plaited hair.

Initiation into adulthood

For a Masai youth, cir-
cumcision marks the end of
childhood and entry into
manhood. When this happens
he becomes a young warrior
and leaves the camp for his
initiation. In times gone by, all
the young warriors would
together receive full training
from the older men. The
young warrior would do no
work, instead plaiting his hair
and colour it with yellow
ochre then going off to steal

Houses in Masai villages are covered with mud and cow dung.

animals from neighbouring herds and trying to provoke a confrontation with a lion. On returning victorious from his single combat with the king of beasts, the warrior would don the lion's mane, thus entering the ranks of adult men. Throughout the African savannah it is said that Simba ('the lion' in Swahili) was so afraid of the Masai that he would change direction if he saw their long silhouettes armed with a single lance.

Other African peoples respond differently to the lion

The 'indomitable lions' are the national football team of Cameroon.

The Bushmen of the Kalahari Desert hunt with a bow and poisoned arrows, whose tip is dipped in snake or spider's venom, or else in poison from plants. As the venom's effect is not always immediate, the hunter has to use all his skills to track the wounded animal in a hunt that may last for several days. The man's prey, mortally weakened by its injury, is then vulnerable to being eaten by large predators, who offer serious competition to the hunter. Dealing with animals such as the lion is therefore part of

African lions represent a disruptive element for human societies, preying on the herdsmen's cattle and competing with hunters by taking their wounded victims.

▼ The Lion Child is an African tale filmed by French director Patrick Grandperret and recounts the adventures of a ten year-old boy, Oule, and his friend Lena. The boy is born into a village protected by lions and is brought up by a young man called Sirga, who teaches him the secrets of the jungle. Oule and Lena are then abducted and imprisoned in the palace belonging to the Lord of the Highlands. They manage to escape using the knowledge Oule has acquired and return to the land of the lions, where Sirga is waiting for them.

The nomadic Bushmen, who are hunters and gatherers, live in the Kalahari desert, which straddles the borders of Botswana, Namibia and South Africa.

Sun City' park in South Africa is decorated with statues of animals.

hunting and, on reaching puberty, young Bushmen are allowed to follow their fathers into the bush to learn what to do: 'Face the lion, don't look away, but never look into the eyes of a leopard'. Bushmen legends tell of clever jackals that just manage to escape a grisly death, while big lions are held up to ridicule.

Bushmen are highly skilled with the bow and hunt with poisoned arrows. They sometimes track a wounded animal for several days.

Beneath the representation of the sun, the two lions painted on the wall of the tomb of Inherkaou in Thebes represent the two lions of the horizon, Yesterday and Tomorrow.

Egypt's most famous sphinx is carved into a rocky outcrop below the pyramid of Chephren, pharoah of the ancient empire, and has always interested pilgrims and travellers. In the 18th century it was thought to consist of a woman's head on a lion's body and assumed to link the zodiac signs of Virgo and Leo. When it was discovered, only the head was sticking out of the sand. The shape of the lion's body lying down was not fully recovered from the sand until 1866.

Lion gods and monstrous lions

The Egyptians were carving lions on the bas-reliefs and tombs of their pharoahs 4500 years ago. The sphinx, a grave enigmatic creature, has a human head on a lion's body. The sphinx of Chephren, 39 metres long and 17 metres high, was erected near the three great pyramids of Giza, near Cairo.

For more than 4500 years the sphinx has guarded the tomb of the pharoah.

The significance of the sphinx

Smaller sphinxes also line the route from the temple at Luxor to the one at Karnak. The exact significance of the figure of the sphinx in Ancient Egypt remains very mysterious, although it appears that it may have solar origins. One thing is certain: the Egyptian sphinx is always male, unlike the sphinx of Greek mythology. It is thought to have guarded the entrances to the funerary sanctuaries of Egypt's rulers and some Egyptologists see it as a symbol of the power and wisdom of the pharoah, who is represented here as a guardian of eternity.

These strange figures, half-human, half-animal, on the walls of the tomb of king Seti I in the Egyptian Valley of the Kings represent the constellations.

The lion's mane on Egyptian statues is a truly majestic headdress.

Sekhmet, the lioness who punished humanity

On one of the gold sarcophagi in the tomb of king Tutankhamen there is a text which tells of a time when Ra, the sun-god creator, was still living on earth. Seeing that he was getting old, says the text, human beings started to plot against him. Ra realized this and at once sent his daughter Hathor to wipe out humanity. To do this, the avenging goddess turned into the furious lioness Sekhmet, meaning 'the powerful one', a terrifying creature symbolizing war. She pitilessly massacred many people, wallowing voluptuously in blood. After this painful episode, the Egyptians regarded contagious diseases as Sekhmet's chosen messengers. Her priests were renowned for their healing powers and were always ready to sacrifice criminals to their goddess.

The tomb of the sons of Ramses III is decorated with a jackal and a lion.

The marmorean statue of a sphinx, representing king Thutmose and built by king Menes in the town of Memphis, Egypt's most ancient capital.

Among the other celebrations on Singapore's national day, a lion dance takes place in the 'City of the Lion', following a Chinese tradition maintained by the island's people.

A symbol throughout Asia

Though now threatened with extinction, the Asian lion has made its mark on the culture and art of this vast continent. Lions are omnipresent in traditions from India to Japan and also play a very important symbolic role in China, a country which has never had a lion population.

The hill of Sagaing, near Mandalay in Burma, is home to about a hundred buddhist monasteries. Its entrance is guarded by two imposing lion statues.

On the island of Java in Indonesia, Hindu and Buddhist traditions still have a strong presence in the sacred frescoes decorating many temple walls.

The acrobats of the Beijing circus sometimes wear lion costumes.

The Asian lion has long been called king of the beasts in India, where it is has become a symbol of human power and sovereignty. In ancient Indian civilization, to fight a lion was considered the ultimate test for anyone with pretensions to command. Gradually this practice evolved into the more symbolic and less dangerous action of wearing a lion's skin.

A brilliantly coloured monumental lion stands guard in front of the pagoda of Kuthodaw, one of the many Buddhist temples in the Mandalay area.

During the Indian independence celebrations the country's majestic emblematic lions grow to gigantic size.

The emblematic lion of India

Two thousand years ago the Indian emperor Asoka in his great city of Sarnath took the lion as his emblem and had an effigy made representing four lions back to back. Today the modern republic of India has once more adopted this ancestral symbolism for its coat of arms, asserting its total sovereignty as an independent state, adding the motto, 'Truth alone triumphs'.

The throne of the Maharajah Gaj Sing is decorated with golden lions.

In Indian mythology, the lion is the sacred mount of many divinities. A lion helped the goddess Durga in her struggle against the demon Mahisasura.

Vishnu's finest!

The god Vishnu, keeper of the cosmos in Indian mythology, may appear in different forms, both human and animal, called 'avatara', meaning descents or incarnations. Among the ten avatara described in the Hindu tradition is Narasimah, the man-lion, a combination of the best of the higher creatures – human beings – with the best of the lower creatures – lions – embodying the best of creation.

India adopted lions as its national emblem in 1950.

The Asiatic lion has suffered so badly from hunters and human activity in its traditional territories that today its population has dwindled to a few hundred animals.

Apart from zoos, where a few animals are on show in captivity, the Gir national park in India is the only place in the world where the lion of Asia can still be seen.

The goddess Durga proudly rides a fierce lion on the battlefield.

India's last lions

Despite its undoubted glory in India, the Asian lion has almost disappeared from that country. In the early 20th century the last region in which it was still to be found, Gir, in the state of Gujarat on the west coast, was hit by a terrible famine combined with a serious drought. All living things were affected by the lack of food, which drove the region's lions to attack human beings weakened by hunger. This behaviour, motivated by the imperative to survive, unleashed massive reprisals, leading to a catastrophic reduction in lion numbers. In 1910 the region had a population of barely 100 individuals. The last lions in Gir were saved from total extinction by the protection granted to them by a local ruler, the Nawab of Junaghad, who effectively banned all lion-hunting on his lands. The lion population of Gir was then able to increase. After the declaration of independence in 1947, the conservation policy started by the Nawab of Junaghad was continued and strengthened by the Indian government, which was well aware of the vulnerability of the lions' last sanctuary.

The Assyrian demons were winged lions or bulls with human heads.

Human king against animal king

In the Assyrian civilization of the first millenium BC, fighting wild beasts was also one of the king's duties. Wild animals represented the untamed forces of nature, evil and chaos, in contrast to the sovereign, whose role was to maintain good order in the world. The lion, the most

Nepalese drawings of lion-hunters riding elephants show that lions were present throughout Asia in times gone by.

The gate of Ishtar, the main entrance to the city of Babylon, was clad with blue varnished bricks, on which a relief portrayed the emblematic animals of the most important gods of the Assyrian pantheon. These were the lion of Ishtar, goddess of love and war, the dragon of Marduk, Babylon's chief god, and the bull of Adad, the storm-god. The gate of Ishtar was the starting point for the great processional route which led across the city to the palace of Nebuchadnezzar.

Today many monuments in the ruins of Babylon, ancient capital of Mesopotamia, bear witness to the city's former splendour.

noble and dangerous of animals, was the preferred opponent in this symbolic struggle.

A lion's tribulations in China

Although the lion is not the king of the animals in China, where the title goes to the tiger, it is a sacred animal of great importance in Chinese mythology, representing power and courage. Originally there were

The gate to the Hall of Supreme Harmony in Beijing is guarded by a lion.

no lions in China. The first individuals were given as presents to the Chinese emperors by the rulers of states in western Asia, who wanted to trade with merchants on the silk route. After this it became traditional to have a pair of stone or bronze lions guarding the entrance to palaces and large buildings for protection as well as decoration. They were also placed in front of Buddhist temples, where they served the same function

A stone lion stands at the entrance to the marble temple in Bangkok.

In Burmese astrology, the day on which a person is born corresponds to an animal: the tiger for Monday, the lion for Tuesday and the elephant for Wednesday.

The many palaces and temples within the famous Imperial City or Forbidden City in Beijing are protected from evil spirits by lions.

The Barong, a mythical creature present in the folklore and beliefs of the Indonesian island of Bali, is a powerful and protective figure, similar in face and shape to a lion. The traditional dance of the Barong is performed by dancers wearing masks and costumes and stages the eternal struggle between the forces of Good, represented by theBarong, and Evil, embodied by the terrible Rangda, a creature bringing death and destruction. The Barong protects human beings against the Rangda's malevolent influence.

The Balinese carve lions, known as Singa, into the volcanic rock.

combined with the defence of the faith and of holiness. In these pairs of Chinese lions, the male is on the right, often shown playing with a ball symbolizing the cosmos. On the left, the female protects her cub with her paw. In the Buddhist tradition, lions have a supernatural strength and are considered as the protectors of holy beings, who sometimes ride on them.

The lion's dance

An old Chinese story tells how a strange creature appeared in China a long time ago, devouring and terrorizing both people and animals. This monster, as fast as it was ferocious, was called 'nien', a name similar to the Chinese word meaning 'year'. Neither the fox nor the tiger could fight the 'nien', so as a last resort the Chinese called to the lion to help them. The lion shook his mane, threw himself on to the 'nien' and wounded it. The 'nien' ran off with its tail between its legs, without however forgetting to announce its imminent return and vengeance. A year later it reappeared. This time the lion could not help as he was too

On important occasions, such as Singapore's national day, the tradition of the Chinese opera, with its actors in elaborate costumes and make up, combines with the lion dance.

In the Beijing opera, each detail of the costume or set is significant.

busy guarding the emperor's palace. So the villagers decided they would pretend to be the lion. They made a lion costume out of bamboo and cloth. Two men slipped inside it and approached the 'nien' stamping and roaring like a real lion. The terrified monster ran away again. Since this glorious day, at each Chinese New Year people dance the lion dance to chase the demon away until the next year. The lion dance was first performed under the

Han (205–220 AD) and reached its height during the T'ang dynasty (716–907 AD). Since then it has spread as far as Korea and Japan. Besides the classic festivities in celebration of the Chinese New Year, the lion dance is also performed during important events such as the opening of a restaurant or at a wedding. If it is well-executed this spectacular dance is guaranteed to bring prosperity, luck and happiness.

China has never been home to the lion, yet there is an ideogram to represent it.

During the lion dance, a dancer carries the head at arm's length, expressing the animal's moods by moving its eyes, mouth and ears.

The winged lion, companion to Saint Mark and protector of Venice, stands out against a starry sky on the upper part of the clock tower in Saint Mark's Square.

A figure in Europe

From the mythological stories of Greece to Roman circus games, the ancient civilizations of the Mediterranean basin gave the lion pride of place. The Middle Ages also frequently used the figure of the king of beasts to give symbolic weight to the power of sovereigns.

At the centre of the Alhambra, former palace of the Moorish kings in Granada, Spain, lies the famous Court of the Lions, with its fountain supported by twelve marble lions.

Daniel, hero of the book of the Bible that bears his name, was unjustly cast into the lions' den; however, to everyone's surprise, he came out miraculously unharmed.

The king of the beasts often appears in Jean de la Fontaine's fables.

Herodotus, the Greek historian of the fifth century BC, mentions the presence of lions in the north of Greece at the time when the armies of king Xerxes were passing through the area in 480 BC. The lions attacked the troops and killed several camels. Aristotle's treatise, *The History of Animals*, written in the fourth century BC, contains numerous observations on the lion and proves that there were lions in Palestine and Macedonia until 322 BC.

Legendary monsters

One Greek legend tells among other things of the arrival of a mythical creature at the gates of the city of Thebes. This monster, called Sphinx, or 'strangler', had the head of a woman, the body of a lion, the wings of an eagle and a serpent's tail. No one could enter the city without passing in front of it. It would then ask the mysterious question, 'Who has four legs in the morning, two at midday and three in the

The sphinx has retained its fascinating power since ancient times.

Cybele, the Greek goddess of the earth, had power over the wild beasts and is often depicted riding in a chariot pulled by lions.

evening?' Any visitor who failed to answer was torn to pieces by the monster without further discussion. For months no one could approach Thebes without rashly taking their life in their hands; however, eventually a young man called Oedipus decided to try his luck. The Sphinx posed him its riddle and, after a brief moment's thought, he gave the correct answer, 'Man. He walks on four legs in the morning of his life, stands on two legs at its midday and walks with the aid

This sacred vase showing a lion's head was found in Mycenae (16th century BC).

The monstrous chimera had a the head of a lion, a goat's body and a dragon's tail and spewed out terrible flames. It was defeated by the hero Bellerophon, riding Pegasus.

The struggle to the death between the legendary Hercules (also known as Heracles) and the terrible lion of Nemea ended in victory for the Greek hero.

The five lion statues of the famous Terrace of the Lions were erected in the late seventh century BC on the island of Delos, at the heart of the Greek Cyclades archipelago.

The lionesses' gate stands at the entrance to Agamemnon's palace in Mycenae. Over the vast lintel stand two heraldic lionesses on either side of a sacred pillar, representing the great goddess and conferring holiness on the building. Though these sculptures are somewhat damaged today, they retain all their majesty. Other works of the archaic period figuring lions include the tomb of the lion at Xanthos, and the lions pulling Cybele's chariot on the frieze of the treasure of Siphnos.

Centuries of wear have not diminished the majesty of the carved lions of Delos.

of a stick at its evening'. With the riddle solved, the Sphinx flew into a terrible rage, fell from its rock and was killed.

The lion of Nemea

Heracles, illegitimate son of the god Zeus and the mortal Alcmene, was pursued all his life by the jealous Hera, Zeus' official wife. Having killed his wife and children in a fit of madness caused by Hera, Heracles was condemned by the Olympian gods to serve Eurystheus, king of Tirynth, for 12 years. The king ordered him to carry out 12 tasks, all of which the hero managed to complete. His first challenge was to fight the lion of Nemea, a monstrous animal made invincible by its skin, which had mythical powers and could resist all weapons. During the fight, Heracles, who had made himself an enormous club, stunned the gigantic lion before strangling it. Having beaten the lion of Nemea, he only had to skin it. The hero used the animal's own claws to cut through the precious pelt, which he then made into a tunic which made him invincible in his turn.

Bread and circuses

Ancient Rome made great use of the lion, the universal symbol of strength, to assert its power. For example the ferocious beasts participated in the triumph of victorious Roman warriors, chained to their chariots. Thus Pompey celebrated his many victories by having 600 lions march in procession beside him. His rival in Rome, a certain Julius Caesar, had only 400 when he celebrated his own conquests. Apart from these great parades,

The famous circus games took place inside the Coliseum in Rome.

Like Saint Blandine of Lyon, the martyr still celebrated today, many Christians were thrown to the lions and died in terrible agony in front of the Roman public.

OLEO·PRAE·SVMSISTI
EXPEDISTIDEDICASTI·

Captured in North Africa or the Middle East, the lions used in the circus games were starved to increase their ferocity - and their appetite!

lions were used for public entertainment. In addition to the famous gladiatorial combats, the Circus games included the equally famous chariot races and displays by animal trainers. These trainers, who had learned from the Greeks and Egyptians, would show monkeys, bears and even elephants in the arena. The untameable lions on the other hand would be shown chasing rabbits that had been released into the ring, or else martyrs who could thus demonstrate their faith. Sometimes a failed gladiator

Crowds of ordinary Romans would come to watch the shows.

The lions on these two baroque statues do not look very fierce; they are the guardians of the peace that reigns in the royal gardens of Prague.

would try his luck with the lions, thereby gaining a unique opportunity to prove his valour to the Roman public, an audience very keen on violent spectacles.

Medieval Europe

In the imagery of the Middle Ages, the lion embodied both power and justice. To the valiant knights, the lion had strength, courage, pride, nobility and generosity, all the qualities of a true leader. This is why the thrones of medieval kings were often decorated

A lion and a unicorn figure on the royal coat of arms of the British monarchy.

Four lions, each one six metres long, guard the column commemorating Admiral Nelson, one of Britain's heroes, in London.

with lions. Many European chivalric orders were quick to adopt the lion as part of their emblem. The coats of arms of the kingdoms of England, Scotland, Denmark and Norway also included a lion, as did those of cities such as Zurich and Belfort.

A biblical symbol

The king of the beasts is mentioned more than 150 times in the bible. Through his ability to resuscitate his young with his breath alone, he symbolizes the resurrection and for this reason appears on Christian tombs. However, though he may represent Jesus Christ, sometimes known as the 'lion of Judah', he also takes a fearsome, winged shape, symbolizing the Antechrist, herald of the Apocalypse. In this form his qualities are transformed into the faults of ferocity, excess pride, uncontrolled strength and despotism, giving rise to some very disturbing images. A terrible roar sounds from his gaping mouth, showing him as the ally of the infernal powers. The Psalms state moreover that the entrance to Hell is through the jaws of a lion.

Carved lions stand over the entrance to the Palazzo Vecchio in Florence.

The main entrance to the basilica of Saint Mark, patron saint of Venice, shows a lion clasping a Bible, symbol of justice.

▼ The winged lion, closely linked to Saint Mark, has been the mascot of Venice since the time when Venetian sailors, trading with the Infidel, brought the Saint's relics back to the city intact. This provided an opportunity to get rid of Saint Theodore, the patron saint imposed by Byzantium, who was associated with the crocodile. Since that time the lion has appeared throughout the city and on the flags of Venetian ships on the lagoon. On famous Saint Mark's Square, the republic's emblem is represented 14 times.

Captured in his native savannah for the entertainment of the American public, the lion's role as his tamer's partner and foil made him a reluctant star.

A star in the USA

Lions have penetrated every aspect of American culture, which feeds on exoticism and spectacle. From zoos to circuses, literature and film to cartoons and television series, the wild and beautiful lion creates fear and fascination throughout the United States.

Prudence and Fortitude, two majestic pink marble lions carved by sculptor Edward Clarks Potter, stand at the entrance to the New York Public Library.

Tarzan the ape-man with beautiful Jane and his monkey Cheetah.

The character of Tarzan was born in 1912 from the imagination of the American writer Edgar Rice Burroughs, who made him the hero of a series of 43 novels. Tarzan has had unprecedented success worldwide, in numerous film adaptations and a profusion of cartoon strips. On many occasions in his most popular incarnations, such as the series illustrated by Burne Hogarth or the films in which he was played by Johnny Weissmuller, the ape-man faces

In the darkened cinemas of 1940s America, the roar of the famous Metro Goldwyn Mayer lion provided an impressive start to the show.

Tarzan's parodic double, George of the jungle, was a cartoon character before transferring his monkey business to a successful live-action movie.

ferocious jungle animals such as crocodiles, snakes, lions and even other apes. The hero often has to fight a lion with his bare hands or armed only with a knife; but of course he always wins his merciless struggle with the beast.

Elsa the lioness

In another mode altogether, in the 1960s all of America was fascinated by the famous story of the friendship between a lioness and a young American

George may wear a loincloth, but he's certainly not as agile as Tarzan!

The wonderful friendship between the Adamsons and Elsa the lioness makes the story invented by Joseph Kessel in his novel *The Lion* seem all the more believable.

woman, Joy Adamson, wife of a specialist in African fauna. The couple lived in Kenya and had adopted an abandoned lion cub. The animal was raised on a bottle and became a superb lioness named Elsa. After being taught to hunt and live in the wild by her 'adoptive parents', she was returned to the savannah, where she rediscovered her predator's instincts. When in turn she gave birth to three 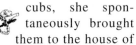 cubs, she spontaneously brought them to the house of

George Adamson's successor, Gareth Patterson, is continuing the struggle.

The film Born Free, made in 1966, brought the story of Elsa the lioness and her human companions the Adamson family to the big screen.

her former masters. Joy Adamson tells the story of her strange relationship with the lions in three books called respectively *Born Free*, *Living Free* and *Forever Free*, which were adapted for the cinema and television. Since then, Elsa has remained a symbol of the readaptation of lions to their natural environment, a process to which the Adamsons devoted their lives. Sadly Joy and George Adamson were murdered by poachers and other animal traffickers, whose activities they had always fought against.

Some lions trained to work in films have become real stars.

Under the biggest big top of all

The great American circuses, such as the famous Barnum circus famed for its larger than life spectacle – gave an important place to animal training. The first of the modern lion-tamers appeared in the early 19th century. Of these, incontestably the finest in America was Van Amburgh, who would impress his audience by dipping his bare arm into a bowl of fresh blood before placing it in a lion's mouth.

To give their audience more of a thrill, circus lion-tamers would risk their lives by entering the animals' cage to take on the show's unpredictable stars.

The lion remains the star of circuses and menageries. Though lion-tamers establish a relationship of complicity and trust with their animals, they are always on their guard, even when they begin training a cub at the age of six to eight months. They maintain a respectable distance, outside a safety zone which varies depending on the animal and the situation. When the trainer enters this zone, he provokes the lion to leap, thereby making it jump on to a stool or through a burning hoop.

In the lions' cage

This period also saw the appearance of the central cage formed by movable bars which could follow the shape of the arena. This important innovation made it possible to exhibit groups of fierce lions without danger to the spectators. Armed with his crop and whip, the trainer would be alone at the mercy of his animals, his armed assistants standing outside the cage ready to intervene. The cage

The lion-tamer's act with her animals pits star against star.

The Big Top by the great Cecil B. de Mille was a spectacular production set in America's famous Barnum's circus.

In the Disney version of Robin Hood, the unscrupulous tyrant King John is shown as a cruel and stupid lion.

itself was linked to the menagerie by a barred corridor. Before these few elementary safety precautions were introduced, lion-tamers settled for simply presenting their animals in menageries, where they moved from cage to cage for the onlookers' pleasure.

The lion as Hollywood star

Apart from Metro Goldwyn Mayer's famous lion, whose roar marks the start of a great number of cult films of the

Clarence, the 'cross-eyed lion', star of the television series Daktari.

A traditional 'baddie' among lion kings, the terrible Scar is an unscrupulous schemer who kills his own brother in order to seize his throne.

The Lion King, a spectacular feature-length animation from the Disney studios, was inspired by an ancient traditional legend from Africa. King Mufasa, an all-powerful lion, reigns wisely over the African highlands. His jealous brother Scar causes his death, which he blames on Simba, the cub destined to inherit the throne. Scar sends the young lion into exile. When he grows to adulthood, Simba returns to drive out the usurper and avenge his father's memory. The film has been enormously succesful throughout the world.

In the Land of Oz, Judy Garland meets the Scarecrow and the Cowardly Lion.

American cinema, there are many lions who are true Hollywood stars. The series of films in which the champion swimmer Johnny Weissmuller plays the role of Tarzan uses 'bad' lions, who are helpless in the face of the ape-man's bravery. In one of America's favourite films, *The Wizard of Oz* with Judy Garland, we find a timid lion, portrayed by an actor in a lionskin. Lions are of course shown in all their splendour in films about circus life, of which the most famous is probably *The Big Top* by Cecil B. de Mille. During a particularly spectacular scene, the lion-tamer faces a lion that has escaped from its cage. The Disney studios made a major place for lions in the world of animation with *The Lion King*, although one had already appeared in an adaptation of Robin Hood, in which Prince John was represented by a lion who seemed quite shabby compared to his elder brother, Richard the Lionheart. As for Clarence, an old lion with a definite squint, he brought worldwide success to the television series *Daktari*, which was a model of its genre.

LIONS

around the world

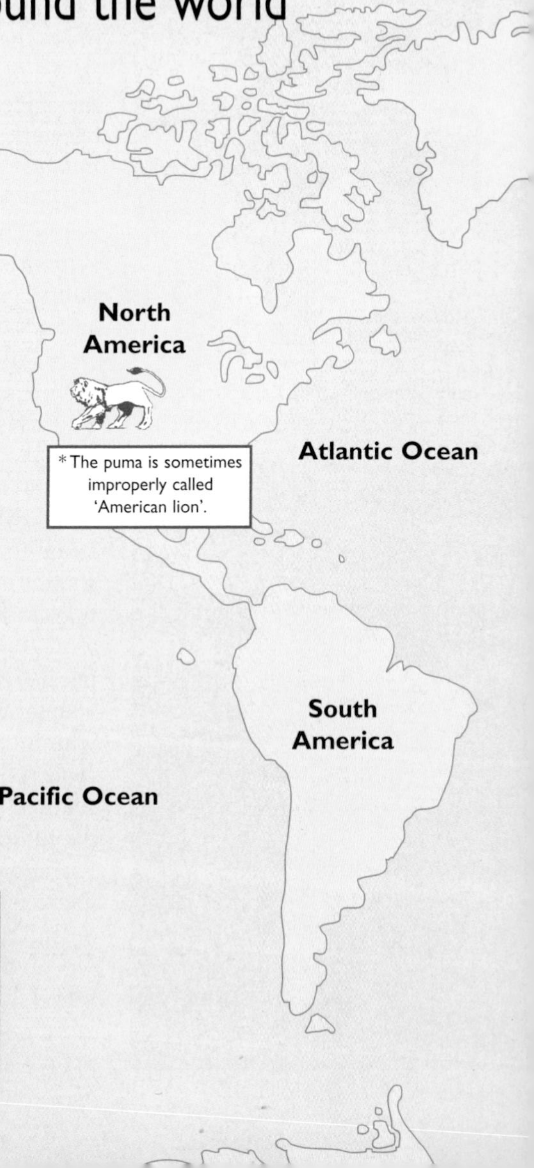

North America

Atlantic Ocean

*The puma is sometimes improperly called 'American lion'.

South America

Pacific Ocean

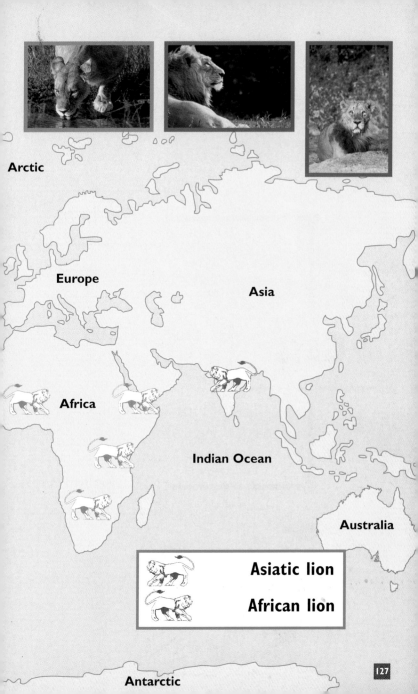

Arctic

Europe

Asia

Africa

Indian Ocean

Australia

Asiatic lion

African lion

Antarctic

LIONS

Principal Species

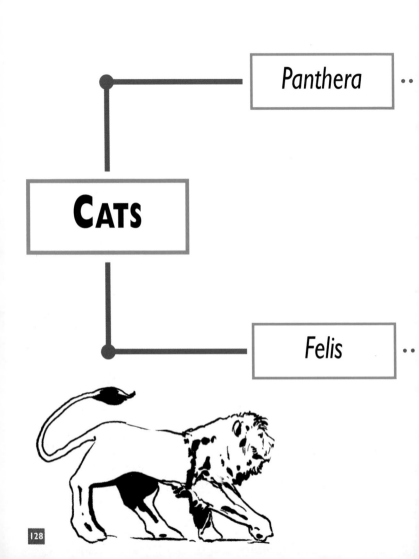

Panthera ··

CATS

Felis ··

The jaguar, the only representative of the panthera genus in the New World, is less known than other large cats.

The Asiatic lion, who only survives in India, and his African brother belong to the same species.

The tiger is the largest living cat on earth. From head to tail, he can measure more than three meters.

The leopard, or panther, is a very discreet large cat who only appears after night fall.

The highly elegant puma is a strong and lively animal. Like a cat, he purrs but never roars.

The wild cat as well as the domestic cat can show themselves as ferocious predators.

Creative workshop

Having studied all of these creatures,
it's time to get creative.

All you need are a few odds and ends and a
little ingenuity, and you can incorporate
some of the animals we've seen into
beautiful craft objects.

These simple projects will give you further
insight into the animal kingdom presented in
the pages of this book.

An original and simple way to enjoy
the wonderful images of the animal kingdom.

Lion toy-hanger

*T*his bright red hanger, decorated with a blue and yellow lion, makes an attractive holder for your favourite toy.

• Photocopy the pattern, enlarging it to the size required.

To make the lion

• Knead the modelling clay to an easily workable consistency. Roll out onto the sheet of glass with the rubber roller (like rolling pastry) until it is about 4mm thick and slightly larger than the pattern.

• Place the photocopy on the modelling clay and press lightly into place with the

palm of your hand.

• Use the cutter to cut the clay, following the outline of the pattern.

• To obtain a smooth finish, pat and smooth the edges of the clay with the flat of the cutter blade.

• Roll a piece of the

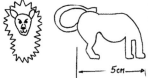

modelling clay into a 'sausage' – about 3cm long x 3mm in diameter – for the tail. Roll another piece into

a small ball for the end of the tail.

• Flatten the front of the lion's body in the mane area and press the mane into place.

• Make a ball (8mm diameter) and shape for the head. Press into place in the centre of

the mane. Make the ears and the eyes and press onto the head using the cocktail stick. Then use the cocktail stick to make 2 holes in the lion's body and 2 in the mane.

• Make another 'sausage' (3mm diameter)

and cut into 5mm sections. Roll one end of each section into a point and fix the sections round the lion's face to fill out the mane.

• Place the lion on a

piece of kitchen foil and bake in the oven (130°C, Gas Mark 4) for 25 minutes.

To paint the lion

• Leave to cool. Use the brush to paint the body and head blue, and the mane and the end of the tail yellow. Leave to dry and then varnish.

To make the hanger

• Cut out the two strips for the hanger from a double piece of material.

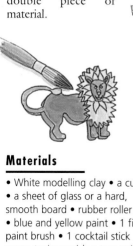

• Sew the ribbon down the centre of the right side of one of the pieces. Place the two pieces together with the right sides facing inwards. Machine them together 1cm from the edge, leaving one end open. Turn the hanger the right side out and sew up the open end. Sew the rickrack braid round the edge of the hanger from the point

where it widens out.
• Ease the ends of the hanger into the tea-towel hooks and hand-stitch into place on the wrong side.
• Sew the lion onto the hanger, about half way up, using blue thread for the body and yellow for the mane.

Materials

• White modelling clay • a cutter
• a sheet of glass or a hard, smooth board • rubber roller
• blue and yellow paint • 1 fine paint brush • 1 cocktail stick
• non-toxic varnish • two strips of material (45cm x 7 cm) cut from an old cotton tee-shirt • 45cm patterned ribbon (1cm wide) with a red background • 90cm yellow rickrack braid • 2 tea-towel hooks
• sewing machine • pink, yellow and blue thread.

Lion stool

*I*f you can draw or paint, you won't be able to resist making this beautifully decorated stool – a worthy tribute to the King of Beasts.

To prepare the stool

• Rub the stool down carefully with sandpaper. Give it two or three coats of white acrylic paint, making sure you rub down between coats.
• Photocopy the designs and then copy each one onto a different sheet of tracing paper.
• Transfer the designs onto the stool.

Painting

• Mix blue and white to paint the sky, shading from pale blue in the mountains to deep blue at the highest point.
• Paint the savanna in Naples yellow and highlight any irregularities in the landscape with yellow ochre mixed with green and brown.
• Paint the lion in Naples yellow and use yellow ochre and brown for the shading on its head and paws.

• Leave to dry and then highlight the mane with short strokes of orange, yellow ochre, red ochre, brown, black and white.
• Paint the eyes in lemon and touch up

with a mixture of yellow ochre and orange. Paint the pupils and the edge of the eyes in black and then outline the eyes with white.

• The lioness is painted with a blend of Naples yellow and yellow ochre. Her jaws are white and her body is outlined in black. Use a blend of black and white to paint her shadow.

• Paint the zebras in white and then paint on their black markings. Their shadows are painted with a mixture of black and white.

• Use ochre for the trees.

Materials

• A stool or small piece of wooden furniture
• white acrylic paint
• sandpaper
• sheets of tracing paper
• paints: blue, Naples yellow, yellow ochre, red ochre, lemon, orange, green, brown, black, white
• brushes

Lion pyjama-case

*T*his majestic golden lion's head is in fact a pyjama-case which can lie on the bed during the day.

Cutting out the pieces

• Copy pieces A, B, (lower jaw) and D (ears) onto the reverse side of the velvet and onto the lining.
• Cut them out, leaving 1 cm all round each shape, then overcast the edges with the sewing machine using zigzag stitches.

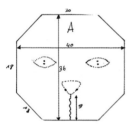

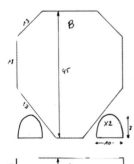

Making the parts

• Pin the velvet and lining pieces right sides together, A to A, B to B and C to C. Machine-stitch around the edges 1 cm in, leaving a 10 cm opening. Use the iron to open out the seams.
• Turn each part right-side-out and iron the seams inside flat.
• Close the openings with small stitches.
• Pass a thread through the bottom of piece C using gathering stitches (see pattern) and pull it to gather in the material and form the muzzle.

Assembly

• Place the bottom of the head A on the table, lining side upwards. Place piece B on top, velvet side upwards, then piece C velvet side upwards. Tack round all the edges so that the pieces do not slip.
• Then sew them together with small stitches all round the edges. Leave 1 cm at the back of the jaws. Hide 2 cm of the braid inside and fasten it there with a stitch.

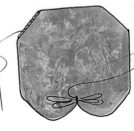

The mane

• Make a 16 cm loop and fasten it with two stitches to the velvet edge of the seam. Repeat all round the circumference of the head to form the mane. Make sure you calculate beforehand how to distribute the length of the braid so that half of it is on top of the head. Finish by tucking the remaining end inside and close up with a few stitches.

The ears

• Assemble and sew the ears with the right side of the velvet to the right side of the lining, leaving the base open so that you can then turn them right side out. Turn down 1 cm towards the inside and sew with small stitches onto each side of the top of piece B, onto the velvet in front of the mane.

The eyes and muzzle

• Roll out a piece of white Fimo modelling clay with a rolling pin until it is 3 mm thick and its sides are 10 x 10 cm. Cut the two eyes out of it with a knife. In the centre of each eye, make two holes close together (like a button) with a knitting needle or an awl.

• Use the brown Fimo to make a triangle for the muzzle, 1 cm thick with sides of 5 cm. Make a hole through the width like a bead. Bake in a medium oven (130°C) for 20 minutes.

When they are cold, decorate them with the paint to make the nostrils and pupils. Stitch them onto piece B.

When you put your pyjamas away inside the jaws, they will fill out the lion's head.

Materials

• A length of old-gold velvet plush 1.10 m wide • A length of lining of the same size in a matching colour • Matching thread • 21 metres of twisted yellow braid 15 mm in diameter • White and brown Fimo modelling clay • A small tube of decorative ceramic colouring in gold • Needles • A sewing machine • An iron

Lion bootees

*K*nitting needles at the ready! With a little felt and a few beads, you can transform traditional bootees into adorable little lions with pearly eyes.

between them on the buttoning strap side to make the upper. There are 32 stitches in all.

Knit four rows of moss stitch then continue 4 cm in stocking stitch for the 10 stitches forming the upper. Set aside

Knitting

• Cast on 23 stitches using the no. 2-knitting needles.
Knit three rows of moss stitch. Decrease 12 stitches to form the strap for buttoning the bootee.

• Set aside the 11 remaining stitches. Cast on 11 stitches (no. 2-needles) and knit three rows of moss stitch, then bring the two pieces together adding 10 stitches

• Pick up the 11 stitches on the right that you had set aside, increase 10 stitches on the right-hand side of the 10 stitches forming the upper, knit the 10 stitches, increase 10 stitches on the left-hand side then pick up the 11 stitches on the left which you had set aside. There are now 52 stitches in all to knit for 6 rows in stocking stitch.

• Then make the sole as follows: set aside 21 stitches on each side then continue knitting the 10 central stitches in moss stitch. Every two rows, knit together the first of the stitches set aside with the first of the 10 central stitches, then the last of the 10 stitches with the first of the stitches set aside. When there are 6 stitches set aside remaining on each side, decrease.

• Knit the second bootee with the buttoning strap on the opposite side.

Sewing the bootees

• Sew the back and heel seams

for each bootee. Make a little button loop at the end of each buttoning strap. Sew a button on each side of the bootee to fasten the strap.

Decoration

• Cut two manes and two triangles for the muzzle out of the piece of felt. Sew them onto the bootees using small stitches. Sew on the little white buttons for the eyes (to give the eyes a more expressive look

you can add a little touch of black paint in the middle of each one).

Materials

• A ball of 'curry' coloured Phildar Egyptian cotton yarn • Knitting needles no. 2 • A small piece of golden yellow felt • Some dark purple tubular beads
• Six small round white buttons

Acknowledgements:

The publishers would like to thank all those who have contributed to this book,
in particular:
Guy-Claude Agboton, Marie-Dominique Arignon, Evelyne-Alice Bridier, Antoine Caron,
Jean-Jacques Carreras, Michèle Forest, Nicolas Lemaire, Hervé Levano,
Marie-Bénédicte Majoral, Kha Luan Pham, Vincent Pompougnac,
Marie-Laure Sers-Besson, Valérie Zuber, Emmanuèle Zumstein

Illustration: Frantz Rey

Translation: Kate Clayton, Trista Selous - Ros Schwartz Translations

Impression: Eurolitho - Milan
Dépôt légal: September 1998
Printed in Italy